I SCREAM
BECAUSE
I'M ANGRY

Copyright © 2019 Erica N. Wortherly, LCSW

First Edition

All rights reserved.

This book, or parts thereof, may not be reproduced in any form without permission from the publisher. Exceptions are made for brief excerpts used in published reviews.

ISBN 978-1933518-43-5

Printed in the United States of America

I SCREAM BECAUSE I'M ANGRY

Written by Erica N. Wortherly

Illusrated by Jamari D. Smith & Shawn M. Abrams, Jr.

A Note to Adults...

This book is intended to be read with a child or group of children to spark dialogue about anger as an emotion experienced by everyone. According to the American Psychological Association, anger is defined as an emotion characterized by antagonism toward someone or something you feel has deliberately done you wrong. Anger can be a good thing. It can give you a way to express negative feelings or motivate one to find solutions to problems.

Adults can help children in several ways.
- Put safety first and help the child get away from the situation to calm down.
- Once the child has calmed down, talk things through. By explaining what occurred, the child is able to engage the thinking part of the brain.
- Ask questions and help the child understand other perspectives.
- Respond with gentleness and compassion. Angry or punitive responses to children's anger add to children's stress when they're already feeling overwhelmed.
- Model appropriate expression. Children learn more from what we do than from what we say. When an adult responds to their own anger in aggressive ways, they not only trigger more anger in children, they also teach that yelling, hitting, or being mean are appropriate ways to behave when angry. Everyone feels angry sometimes, but we want to teach our children that it's possible to feel angry and still treat others respectfully.

To all the children who struggle with

angry feelings and the adults

working with them.

WHY DO I FEEL SO NERVOUS?

Anger is a normal and natural emotion.

It's what we feel when annoyed, frustrated, irritated, stressed, even tired. You can become angry when someone hurts someone you love. It is not good or bad. It is a way of surviving or protecting yourself when something is wrong. You could also be very angry when you don't like other people's beliefs, opinions, and actions.

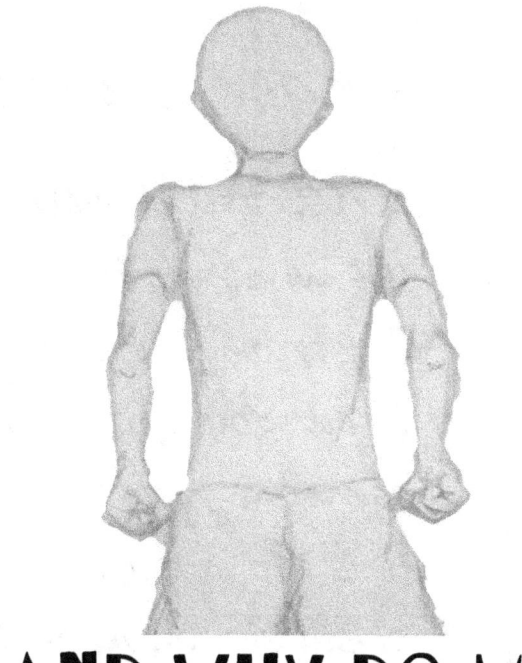

AND WHY DO MY FISTS BALL UP?

Anger causes changes in your body, like fast heartbeat or an adrenaline rush making you want to fight, run away, or freeze. Your cheeks might feel hot. You may throw something. You could start crying. You may even hide.

A trigger is something that leads to anger. It could be many types of reasons. Maybe you didn't get picked in a game. Maybe a teacher yelled at you. Maybe your friend broke your toy. Maybe an adult didn't listen to you.

What is it that makes you mad; that makes you scream or really sad?

WHY DOES MY HEART BEAT BOLDLY...
...AND KEEP MY MIND FROM CALM?

Being sad, lonely, scared, or threatened could also feel like and look like anger.

It is helpful to figure out why you're angry so whatever the problem is can be solved.

ANGER IS AN EMOTION,
A NORMAL PART OF ME.

You are not crazy. You are not bad. You are a person with feelings like everyone else. How you show it might be different and that's okay. We are not able to control our feelings, but we can control how we act. There is a difference between reacting and responding. To react means to behave in a way that could lead to getting in trouble. To respond means to stop and think before you act. That takes some practice. It's best to have an adult practice with you.

IT RISES UP LIKE A FIRE.

IT'S A SHIELD WHEN I FEEL PAIN.

So when anger comes you must try to speak, with your mouth or a picture. You can calm yourself by releasing the energy or it may go away with sleep. Take deep breaths, go on a run or stretch, count items around you or write the words you want to yell. Fighting and screaming is not the only way to get attention. Expressing your anger appropriately should be your mission. Does that mean you will get it right every time? No, but it makes a difference when you know you have tried.

You are human after all and
all humans have emotions.
All emotions work together and help you
know who you are. You are strong and special.
You are not an angry person.

You are a person who
experiences anger...

...and *joy*, sadness, *calm*, fear, confidence, loneliness, and *love*.

I scream because
I'm angry.
I scream for release.
It rises up like fire.
It's a shield when
I feel pain.

Active-The mind and body is active. It will be difficult to calm down immediately. Sometimes it might take longer than other times.

Normal-Anger is a normal and natural emotion with many levels from small frustrations to rage. Determining the cause of the anger through speaking with a trusted adult leads to problem-solving for the future.

Goodness/Grace-Even when something causes anger, good can be found and a lesson can be learned.

Energy-Do something with energy experienced while angry to recover more quickly.

Release-Let it go. Find ways to release the angry feeling by talking, writing, or even crying.

I SCREAM BECAUSE I'M ANGRY
(Tune of "His Eye is on the Sparrow")

Why do I feel so nervous?

And why do my fists ball up?

Why does my heart beat boldly...

...and keep my mind from calm?

Anger is an emotion, a normal part of me.

It rises up like a fire. It's a shield when I feel pain.

I scream because I'm angry.

I scream for release.

It rises up like fire.

It's a shield when I feel pain.

Audio is available on YouTube.

ANGER MANAGMENT SKILLS & STRATEGIES

- Physical Exercise
- Mindfulness/Grounding
- Get Creative
- "I" Statements

All your feelings are natural; it is what you do when you are feeling that way that makes the difference.

Physical Exercise

Benefits

Movement can calm you, energize you, or help you to get rid of excess energy. When you are feeling difficult emotions, you suddenly have a lot of energy running through your body. If you do things to help get rid of the energy, then you will be able to calm down more easily.

Tips

- Squeeze something, a pillow or stressball.
- Go for a walk.
- Do jumping jacks.
- Play.
- Swing.
- Jumprope.

Mindfulness/Grounding

Benefits

Mindfulness is being aware of what is happening in the present moment, not focusing on the the past or the future. It can be done anywhere. Grounding is a way to deal with overwhelming emotions. The goal of these types of exercises is to get from "fight, flight, or freeze" mode back to "rest and digest" mode.

Tips

- Breathe in through your nose and expand the belly, then breath out slowly. This could also be practiced with balloons, bubbles, or a pinwheel.
- Imagine your favorite place.
- Mental grounding is thinking of your favorite things, picturing people you care about, saying the alphabet slowly, or remembering the words to a song you love. It could also be going through the five senses to help remind your of the present; paying attention to what you can see, feel, hear, smell, and taste.
- Physical grounding is running water in your hands, carrying a small object like a stone or shell, or moving or making a fist and releasing it when you need to be brought back to the present moment.

Get creative

Benefits

Using creativity is a great distraction. A child (or adult) may discover a new talent or a new passion. Imagination and creativity are endless!

Tips

- Create abstract art or draw something familiar that brings a smile.
- Write a poem, story, or simply let the words free flow on paper or in a journal.
- Sing.
- Play an instrument-real or not. Make some music.
- Make up a game.
- Make something! Just gather materials like recycling, yarn, paper, markers/crayons and see what you come up with.

"I" Statements

Benefits

"I" Statements are an important communcation skill, especially when there is a conflict. They are clear messages that make it easier for another person to hear what is being said, even when you are angry or frustrated. It helps you to be honest about and take responsibility for our own feelings, and we communicate in a way that encourages positive problem-solving.

Tips

- I feel... (What is your mood? Name an emotion.)
- when... (Describe the specific situation.)
- because...(State the effect on you.)
- and I want... (Stated the action you want taken.)

Example: *I feel* angry *when* people mess with my stuff *because* I can't find it when I need it *and I want* people to ask before taking something that belings to me.

"I" Statements can also be used when experiencing joyful emotions!

Example: *I feel* excited *when* I win my races *because* I practice almost everyday *and I want* to keep getting better.

IT'S A SHIELD

WHEN I FEEL PAIN.

For more information about Erica N. Wortherly or
to order more copies of *I Scream Because I'm Angry* and other books,
please visit www.ericanwortherly.com.

www.ingramcontent.com/pod-product-compliance
Lightning Source LLC
Chambersburg PA
CBHW081737100526
44591CB00016B/2646